Local Hope

Local Hope

Jack Heflin

University of Louisiana at Lafayette Press
2010

"Study Sketch: Ouachita River" by Glenn Kennedy

ISBN 13 (paper): 978-1-887366-98-4
ISBN 10 (paper): 1-887366-98-9

Library of Congress Cataloging-in-Publication Data

Heflin, Jack, 1954-
  Local hope / Jack Heflin.
    p. cm.
  ISBN-13: 978-1-887366-98-4 (pbk. : alk. paper)
  ISBN-10: 1-887366-98-9 (pbk. : alk. paper)
  I. Title.
  PS3558.E417L63 2010
  811'.54--dc22

                                    2010019331

http://ulpress.org
University of Louisiana at Lafayette Press
P.O. Box 40831
Lafayette, LA 70504-0831
Printed on acid-free paper.

For Tami, Jake, Emerson & Wes

Why shouldn't I sing to myself?

Contents

V THE SUPPLICANT

ACKNOWLEDGMENTS

I would like to thank the editors of the following magazines in which these poems previously appeared.

Blue Mesa Review: "Amnesia," "Adolescence"
The Chariton Review: "ClubLand," "A Short Lesson on the Grip," "Bestiary
    for the Back Nine"
Chattahoochee Review: "All the Luck"
Chiron Review: "A Portrait of his Failure as Desire"
Green Mountains Review: "Local Hope"
Gulf Stream: "A Last Visit," *"Ars Poetica,"* "Tenure, an Elegy"
High Plains Literary Review: "Near Viola," "Luck"
The Hiram Poetry Review: "Icarus," "Wind River Canyon"
In Your Face: "Election Year"
Louisiana Literature: "Sadness the Gardener Sows"
The Missouri Review: "The Bad Caddie," "Pan Olympic," "Cat Scan,"
    "Friday Night Fights," "Ash Wednesday"
New Orleans Review: "More Food for the Materialist"
Nimrod: "Carlton Creek Road"
Poetry East: "Domestic"
Poetry Northwest: "The Color of Money"
Red Dirt: "The Cobbler's Journal"
Sonora Review: "The Supplicant"
Willow Springs: "Claryville, Third Sundays in May"

I would also like to acknowledge the Louisiana Division of the Arts for a Fellowship which in part allowed me to complete this collection and the University of Louisiana at Monroe for its continued support.

A special thanks to William Ryan for his readings and suggestions, to my family, of course, for their patience and encouragement, and to Larry Levis and Richard Hugo whose words and memories I will carry with me forever.

I An Easy Touch

ICARUS

Your new wings itching like sunburn
it could just as well have been blue air
into which you leapt but it was only water
the blue city pool and you fell thrashing
through its lovely familiar element
to find no bottom
                    What angel finally
lifted your feather-forgotten arms to touch
again the earth albeit paved with aggregate rock
that pawed your chest when you heaved out
to bear its holy unconcern
How you hungered at its knees
then puked your coughing lovesong to appall

LOCAL HOPE

     From tangle of water oak, from willows torn free upriver
as far as Felsenthal,
                      from bank waste freed from bean field levees,
    from cotton rot, from egrets sipping soggy bottoms, hunting perch,
from cottonmouths tossed like scarves along
     the elegant arms of driftwash,
       from all of this and from the maternal hush of water
distilled before thunder comes the clumsy swish and thump of
     Wal*Mart flipper, extra-large, comes the mumbled
curses, comes the aftershock sighting . . .
                              what's left of him:
thin-shinned splash of a lost olympian gone dunking for God.
       He tugs his goggles, no looking back, floating past
    where he began, kicking a wake of
             arrogance and rage, suspiciously thirsty,
     a blackout draft he'll take all night to drink, cracker thick,
   full of fertilizer and factory scabs, full of mongoloids,
magnolia blooms,
            rafts his fathers built of tar and poker chips,
shattered pitching wedges, sand-bag second mortgages,
     sepia letters, portraits from which no one ever smiles:

All the good men who learned too late they'd never love.

  He chokes it down and bottoms up.
                       He forgets his dream,
but in the fiction-blood of current
       he dreams, he paddles and scrawls,
                  he lunges to the Baptist
deeps,
     past the piscicultural   and the multi-piscicultural,
past whole families fishing for Jesus,
                   past runaways
    picking the bones of a carnival,
  past loggerhead and eel, past moonshine,
roadstand pickled fishfin, past grennel and gar,
                   backstroking, back,
    all the way back,
   birthing himself with each breath

until said host of swollen atavism comes dripping out,
                    pulling its tail,
          slug mud lost beyond the shoreline wrecks rusting phosphorescent
in this paramouric slip of river
                              bruised by flood, bream bed,
          rip-rap glistening in the mythical dawn.
                    Water picks the chassis clean.

                    Farther down from lock and dam, there are only parts,
rear ends and shocks, children dozing over buckets of catfish,
          all you can eat.   The locals laugh
     but like to rub their little heads for luck.

CLARYVILLE, THIRD SUNDAYS IN MAY

There in the marble font of St. Boniface
a blush of votive light, one rounded wave
setting out from where I've dipped my thumb,
an iridescent insect wing and what looks like
callous, or fingernail, just the bluish membrane
of a dream someone might sit up all night
and never tell you.
                                    Tableau of rain and high water,
bells tolling on Kaskaskia, all the good Catholics
blessing their brows, one eye to the levee

. . . and what will the gypsies think this summer
when they return to find us gone, our whole town!
the school house floor, our seats attached,
downstream in the Devenyn's garden?
Mother picked mullein leaves and yarr, a tonic
for their fever, let Queen Eva sit before her mirror
to mix her crayon makeup. I suppose we'll cross the bridge
at St. Mary's Slough, take our typhoid shots
in Chester, but where will we go? Will we come back
on Sundays to see the Captain, swap our lilacs
for lemon candy and barber-pole peppermints,
get to climb the second deck and wave to home?
Home is washed away. Our grand hotel the Tucker
two days held against the current, finally split apart.
Valle Huber's house is gone, and I shall fight against
the devil to fancy the sand boil spewing first
from under Felix Vallery's barn . . .

                                    or is it my own voice
I'm afraid of: drowning down some ruined cistern,
lost where vision leaves me, without breath,
and where lately I have been dreaming again, about you,
wading the ditches, bent over the smallest reward,
an old woman in scarf and brogans
as she climbs the hill to Mass.

                                    for Esther Streiler

CIRCA

In the warehouse of suffering there are many rooms,
rooms of empty numbers, rooms we never want to go inside,
blue rooms rising beyond indifference,
> beyond the nightly count of lies,
beyond the future reliability of the automobile, or the toaster,
or the state department or
> the rooms for rent inside the Kenner House
across the street, where I am also never to go, two dollar a week home
to the shattered renters/lost relatives who have ended there
to retire without peace,
> where someone has opened
the window to the paralytic's room, to let her torment
pass into the street, into that sticky air full of aphids
and green maples.
> *Dink of water* she pleads *dink of water.*
So everyone can hear. A hundred times a day.

Hiding somewhere twisted
in the backyard maple, in my closet among the leaves,
I'm desperate to whistle, no birdsong rock n roll, no sitcom smiling melody
    but shrieking blasts that travel blocks,
> rattling stopsigns and shopfronts.
  The secret's in the seed pods, the minnowed
reeds I work between my teeth,
> screeching like cicadas,
like after-school traffic fish-tailing out of town.

  At the table there's little to say, the TV on, the news,
the lurid rooms of war along the DMZ,
    a man kneeling beside his hut counting on his fingers
the doors he was pushed through to arrive here
  at the waiting room of death.
> *Dink of water*
dink of water. Before sleep I'm bodiless,
strafing low through a darkness of pillows and icy sheets,
a weary hero back from the jungles of unconcern
holding the bluest water in the bluest glass,
    all she can drink . . .
> but for the unshaven louts

who eye me as I go banging out the door.
Dink of water. Some how they've learned to shut her out.

    When not one of them is loafing on his busted wicker,
I go poking through the pissy smelling privets,
looking for my treasured balls I've hit across the road,
thinking I've got thirty seconds, maybe a minute,
but I don't.
                 A whistle, full of spit and spiders, stops me,
lockjawed in its venom. *I've got 'em all inside, all of them.*
Your box of balls.
                 He's got me by the arm and I'm kindly
driven down the hall, where the rooms turn left and right,
the room the widow sprawls inside.
                 I can't bring myself to look,
No water made can take that thirst away, he tells me.
       In the common room
there it is, as promised, a cardboard box of baseballs,
tennis balls, whiffle balls, all mine, waiting on me
the whole time,
            but I still can't move. All around me
the faces swivel from the Motorola,
                      all caught in the spell
of the same quiet, the same news.
    I wear their stares a long time before I leave.

    Outside in a green room beneath the trees,
under the fierceness of beak and eye, suffering rehearsed
      a thousand songs and sang them all by heart.

AMNESIA

But if I turn this way, stripped of even my passion,
without history, I'm waking from a nap in a pickup,
smeared against the door, lost in a caption of twilight

burning in the side mirror, without panic or conscience.
Sweat cools along my temple, inside my ears.
Even the song of the lark is pitched without rumor,

fluent in the forgotten grammar of wind falling
now through leggy fields of fescue, lespedeza.
A few nouns and it all comes back, Rapid City,

the long declension of the plains, the afternoon,
the driver pausing for another lens, another angle
of Nebraska, the sunburnt album some widow

refused to pack, blown up against the rage
of wire and drought. We pick the ruins
near the road, read the mail six decades dead . . .

as if nothing had happened, as if all we had to do
was breathe. O, Lucy, such wickedness. The painted mare
you rode to Valentine froze slick against her stall.

Farther south the emphysemic summer
burns so hot I jog each afternoon for spite,
no orphaned postcard I, my face red as prairie fire,

lightning for the sake of drama only.
Without the wind to laugh my father apes
my frantic pace, he shuffles down the drive

in just his underwear. He wants to smoke
and I can't quit. After supper I go sneaking off
behind the house, lighting up, back to it all,

indifferent to the day far ahead when I recall
the truck that slowed to take a closer look,
and the faces scowling at our rummage.

for Ron Hansen

CARLTON CREEK ROAD

Beyond the radio's inscrutable acappella comes a scream,
neither Latin nor Mozart,
so far away   I feel it first in the flesh of my feet,

the numbing sparks tunneling upward,

groinshock

at the naming of my neighbor's cry—
Jack (like the strike of an axe) *Jack,*

wind-scraped, coughing,
the echo of blood upon my blood.

Out the door and down
the shortcut mile to his cabin,

over slalom
of dead-fall, I dash like a chicken,
hysterical.   How will I find him?

Sunk in a posture of fright,
splintered from fall,

the drooling-beggar bears come back?

I lose a loafer, trip, stagger on, pinching gravel
with my toes, turn the corner to the drive.

No one's home:
No one called my name. Such quiet.
Okay.

For three days I've been alone,
talking to my self, stalking pathos with a pencil
through hours of blurred edges, unusual sleep.

Now this.

In the grip of these racking respirations,

it's a long time before I sit up, relax, sip the thin
Montana air where twilight has lingered
like a cigarette in the hand of my father.

It too darkens quietly to ash.

A shiver runs down the valley,
leaks its way

through barn stave and board slat,
    through shirt-sleeve and scar,
        until everything born of this earth
   whistles visibly in the wind.

ALL THE LUCK

Who's the fool in his underwear
kicking the dead shark she's found in the surf?
From under a floppy Panama he snarls at the camera,
but he'll do anything she asks,
                              so over the washed-out logs,

the oily perch of pipers, they come stumbling down the beach,
posing here and there, nudging starfish out to tide, scavenging
jokes, evicted invertebrates, limpets, coral and rattled conch,
coins of polished wood,

                    a sack of charms
to light their inland windowsills,
charms they'll dust and charm they'll lose and turn
and never touch again.

———————

The last bus leaves at dusk,
second class, a fifty peso ride to Vera Cruz,
a handful of change you rattle down a phone,
price of a sweet bread melting on your tongue.

———————

You climb aboard in Whitefish,
Christmas Eve, kicking the snow from your Sorel boots,
ride the trainlong dusk through Glacier Park,
Lake MacDonald:
                    Anemone light along the peaks,
the moon blowing west in the window
lighting valleys down the Divide, Marias Pass, Browning,
someone's drunken tongue stuck to a stock rail,
a Buick full of Blackfeet fleeing east, black ice,
salmon spooked from a cutbank.
                              Across the aisle
the marine recruit is cleaning reefer.

You turn away but there it is—

    beneath your light, your novel, your sorrow.
Sleepless, insouciant, Montana tilts in the window,
filling with Cadillacs and ranch hands,
starfish and whiskey, disheveling road houses,
sand sharks swirling through the snow,
smug with evolution.

                   You were a man of solid spine,
tickled with hallucination, assured your only failure
was your innocence. Farther east, the frozen Milk,
the ghost of old Joseph stooping for a drink.
At dawn, a drunk fogging a phone booth,

Tell me you love me.
I don't love you.

———————

         Into the cookie tin go the arrowheads
wrapped in socks, obsidian points you tuck in jewelry boxes
stuffed with cotton, toy guns and toy soldiers, two onyx elephants,
the silk screen panda nibbling bamboo, ivory billiard balls
you'd learned to juggle:

                   All the luck you couldn't live without.

    And in the framed eye of the palomino
you read it all, the last words, wrong looks,
the sand dollars stuck to a window pane you'd break with your fist,
blood running to your elbow . . .
                  a green hat full of photographs
curling in the flames of a Weber grill,
no smile, no subterfuge,
your frozen palms, your frozen face.

———————

The waves come lunging in
like drunks at daylight, farther out,
two ducks corked above a school of blues,
on the pier, anglers staring down their lines,
like poets, fishers of the lost,
water the color of coins that taste
like sugar on the bread of your tongue.

———————

If you were suddenly somebody
else, startled with a reflection in a window, reaching
toward the glass, to the whorled snails, shining cowrie shells,
the crusty seahorse come to life,

a little unsold self forgotten.

Tell me you love me,
I don't love you.

WIND RIVER CANYON

All the poems I've begun for you
I never wanted to write,
not the ones that brought you into my arms,
or even your crying over the tulips
in the window thirty years ago.
But I have no photograph of this
and my memory blurs like the wind
bending the notes of a lark over acres of prairie.
In the photo in front of me,
taken where the Great Plains heave into the Rockies,
you're partnered with the Wind River Canyon.
Two miles behind you
the river falls upon your shoulder,
no wider than your arm, though boulders
big as Winnebagos tumble in its bed.
The wind is blowing east toward the sun
and appears to be shoving you
out of the picture, as if even then
you knew of your absence years later.
In your eyes there is question,
something you want to tell me, and it is all right
if it too is left in the wind.

A PORTRAIT OF HIS FAILURE AS DESIRE

*to be away from home and yet to feel oneself
everywhere at home; to see the world, to be at
the center of the world, and yet to remain
hidden from the world . . .*

-Baudelaire

Beyond the millrot at the end of the lake
he kicks at something in the mud

then bends to pick it up, a bone to
diagnose he smiles when *Doctor* has the time.

Hungry, he wanders on to linger
in the truck stop mirrors or the caught looks

of strangers before he leaks off through the trees,
his laughing stuntman shadow

leading him through his lies to the entrance ramp.
He wipes a crusty frost from his feet.

In the headlights he's just an extra
on the set, thumb out, inattentive, unpaid,

a bit of backdrop there beside the road,
map of the devil's backbone spilling at his feet:

A billboard, its child's face pocked by winter,
a three-legged dog hopping off through the rain . . .

To find me now will cost you everything.

Go ahead, he says,
taste it. Crystal icing in the valley of his palm,

17

the unruly river rising under his tongue
Out of the bag the blues pour out: the busted levees

spilling over his chin: the Gasconade, the Bitterroot,
the Ouachita, and when he's had enough, he sleeps,

oddly quiescent, in a bag decorated with lassos, with cowboy hats,
with semen dreams. All this near the Calcasieu,

he remembers, his neck locked in a cramp,
the world gone green with duck weed,

the official color of distraction. Turkey buzzards
nod in the cypress, thoughtless, disheveled,

big as suitcases, then fall with a slap on the water.
He wakes, absorbed, as if the camera caught him

————

unaware, his eyes stitched with light. Look closer
you'll find a morning's square inch measured

a sentence at a time between the baby's naps
and the cries that carry him back, like a rhyme

spinning from a carousel above the crib.
In this clause he slaps the tarp across the trailer,

he loads the last box, the bikes, the Weber pit.
Through his hands the long rope comes

to strap the load, to tie it off, eyelet to anchor.
But he's not going anywhere. Out the window,

out there, a cemetery orchard, the cedar fruit
no man could parse, no knife could pare.

————

His eyes blur in the side-mirrors,

unraveling at the vaguest shift in weight,

or suggestion that none of this is true . . .
back home, the luckless recluse,

abstracted, irresponsibly wise,
a hand walking the borders of a map.

———————

Deliberately lost, he's just running
where his legs lead him, almost flying,

the truth no one dares, the long strides,
and yet he stumbles, his chin aches.

He rises, lighter, more loosely assembled
in this wilderness of the ordinary,

along ragged seams between neighborhoods,
down spiraling paths available to no one else,

that no one sees, where gardens sleep, mulched
against winter, unencumbered, like the homeless.

Only in the known joys of exhaustion
does it come upon him, such complete exit.

How long had he been dozing in the warm
grass behind the hill, cheating the track coach?

———————

Up the yellow maple on Main he could see
down the street the parade just turning the corner,

the silly floats. The Class of '59—*Your Road to Success:*
a cardboard Cadillac, all pink and feathered,

topped with a queen. He rides beneath her,
under the seat, the engine, the center of an attention

never seen, there in the crepe-paper dim,
turning the axle and wooden wheels.

for Chris McCandless

AN EASY TOUCH, AFTER READING MONTALE

He staggers out of an alley of cans behind the Ox,
a half-eaten sports page, a ragged biscuit,

some keno tickets stuffed in his shirt. Missoula 8am.
The same dude who tagged me for a dollar

as I staggered out of The Hat last night.
At least I remember. Not him.

He thinks I'm just a lucky touch
for a cool drink his little daydream has lead him back to.

The secret breath of all this shit.

No domandarci la formula che monde possa appariti

Should I ask him to translate?

Codesto solo oggi possimoi dirti

Montale!

Cio che non siamo, cio che non vogliamo

Your white horse is riding
the runways of twilight.

il mio sogno di te non e finito.

When I raised my hand
I was only shifting the load
of these groceries. Not my guilt.
No place to land your ruins.

for Wm. Ryan

II The Color of Money

no matter where it's mined . . .

TOURING THE INTERIOR

You see them from the road,
lounging on summer wicker,
disdaining in their ease,
life-size dolls on sale at twenty bucks:
an orange-eyed witch, Santa
and Mrs. Claus, lumpy grandpa
in pipe-cleaner spectacles, a horseshoe
of yellow hair above each ear.
The owner never learned to spell: *Fragil Murchindize.*
In her land of dollar hymnal fans
Christ our Savior opens to everyone,
everything's for sale: the porcelain frogs,
the church pew fans, the ashtrays of tourists
condemned to home—chipped vistas
of Stone Mountain, Buxom Ozark Daisie Mae
dressed in bottle caps, begging for a smartass butt.
Over the sewing shop out back
she warns you *Do Not Entur,* loosely translated,
your trespass to another tongue. For a laugh
you chauffeur grandpa across the river
to a bar so broken down the lovenames
carved above the bathroom stool must be decades dead
or impotent, clutching the mattress hearts
laid down beside them, sadness just clear enough to spell.
Sunset wades its Pentecostal hair in Old Man River,
on you a splashy glare you squint to shield,
alive among the many arms waving to arms
waving from balloons hung like colored balls
in the air above Natchez. Time to fish grandpa
from his dozing, rough him up a bit,
make him tell a joke before you hit the road.

for Richard Hugo

TENURE, AN ELEGY

—O Lord please don't let me be misunderstood.
-Eric Burden

On the phone I barked a bluefire spit I'd fed
with epithets and *fuckits* all the drive home,

all part of a little speech I was preparing
for the VP of Business Affairs.
As I stood there, on hold,
managing my anger like a union rep, like an adolescent,
I fought the mail piled on the counter—

bills, solicitations, credit card come-ons, the colored
flyers full of tillers and chickens, the grease-free sex
a kitchen remodel promised everyone but me.

All fell like targets before the market eye.

I opened, then, in that splenetic moment
the Bible of the academic fabulist—*Poets & Writers.*

And there it was, your name *In Memoriam.*

My guts tumbled, I almost fell.
He'll speak to you now.

Huddled in the basement of my breathless grief
I stuttered my stupid complaint.

Reading Lorca, poem after poem,
laughing, inhaling voluminously
the smoke from a Marlboro,
you praised what alone was worth the labor
of the fool.

How about a loan?
the VP offered, *I could right you a check.*

My ass slackened from around my ears,

essential anatomies of the poet's apparel.

I was broke, just out of school,
but learning a trade I had managed to romantically ennoble.

From you I learned the happy insecurity of art,
the way style dresses the man
who's never coming back.

for Larry Levis

FRIDAY NIGHT FIGHTS

This is years ago,
before I learned to just double up
   and bruise,
         when running was still my best defense,
something visceral, pheromonal:
                  atavistic *vamonos.*
   Organs huddled in their little caves.
Horns blared, hardened proteins beat their cell walls
     with a dread so thick
I felt it swell along my ears,
               run down
   my yellow back, before I leapt ahead
of danger's fist, of a logic my body argued
   I had no capacity to deny,

         and I felt it now, old enough
   to understand the coward's flight,
crouched beneath the kitchen window
   for her to break it off with Mister Ex.
                    Grow up!
she screams and slaps
       a pan across the sink.

   If he doesn't touch her, I tell myself,
   I'm not going in. I was trying to be large about it,
      seeing his angle, a man merely brought up
against an awkward transition,
         but I wished they'd leave the kitchen—
skewers and metal racks, knives and rolling pins . . . .

A strange slow-motion settles through the dark,
      the camera zooms from above to the student slums,
to an acid blue shack the corner of Auburn and 2nd,
   inside a man and a woman,
           another man outside, noticeably slighter,
tiptoeing on a pile of bricks.

   A shout. The door shuts—slam-*fuck*—
      the two sounds so timed, the door, the verb,

like lip-syncs in a spaghetti western.
     The reel jerks, stalls, and in the second
it takes to look away from the lovers
                              melting across the screen,

          that still, almost holy, moment
               before violence,

                         when the director falls upon his knees
               and crawls toward the bodies
bristling their ancient defense, millenniums of bone
          and brush retaking the bald plateaus.

He's tired of talking, off comes his watch—
                              yes, sadly, sure sign
he wants to fight, but with a gesture to restraint,
     some fratboy allegicance to ease. No anarchist
so I breathe, loosen my grip on the brick,
                              but he lunges,
     enraged mammal defiled by love,
          Camel Lights tumbling from his shirt.
He has me an easy fifty pounds.
                              I sling a punch
     that thuds like mud against his shoulder.
I'm a chickenshit-meddling-candyass coward, he says.
                                        Yeah, yeah.

     What I am is crabbing across the drive,
               dipping and spinning
like a skipped rock, dodging his wild punts.

          We're in the street now,
legging it down Auburn, almost a sprint,
                         and I feel good,
like I could go a few miles.
                    I keep him behind me
a couple cars back until I hear him panting,
     let off to a lope,
take the left on Louisville.
                    Midnight,
no traffic,
     the road to ourselves.

I could be running springbuck by moonlight
toward a cliff ten thousand years ago.

                         A few more blocks
and I'm walking a bad dog back
       from the hunt. Up ahead

                  the centuries whirl
in colored cop-car lights
      that wait to hear our stories.

The Color of Money

Money is unfortunately the color of grass, pine needles, the shade beneath these elms, even the eyes of some red-headed women, which we can never own, and green's the color of the dingy slough near the Ouachita where I dug a quarter from the dirt, skipped it over the duckweed and bream beds, over the diving loggerheads, the mudfish, all the way to the deep end under the levee. Under this blue, invisible sky I've sprawled and grown mulish, like Panama, staring at the limos on the back of this ten dollar bill. Look at them, stalled forever at the curb of the Treasury, and if the woman the artist has frozen there, the one on the sidewalk waiting her car, if she has red hair and the careless gestures of the rich who've abandoned the republic for Long Island, I still have my hometown which belongs at least to several people. Gib End let us in to name the pigeons scratching his attic. He owned a hotplate and the rotten screen on his back door. His name is not etched on currency. There's still a little honor for the poor. Chivalry has died, the scoundrels have lived and the green paper land under the flag is sacred: it's where I've come to total my debt, it's what I find at my feet. Ah, my green republic, you need me. I'm rubbing the mud from the face of a president.

THE APPRENTICE

. . . nothing to lose but their chains

All morning under waspy eaves he had balanced, brush in hand, bucket coat-hangered to a spongy ladder, but lucky at least to be out of sight, high in these musty caverns from where he could measure his poor man's block of American dream. *Ya mist de endt dar. No dat dar!* It's the owner, the banker's widow. On Friday—a day so far away, to travel there he should have left last night—she'll press the ten twenty-dollar bills into his palm like some tax he'd levied upon her grief. But this is Tuesday, her day to righteously wait in her garden chaise and find mistake with him—her daydreamer apprentice idler—who's just now learning to suffer while he works, who leans out, dabbing primer near a slathered board, condemned he somehow knows he must return to, year upon year to freshen its dulled marxist lustre. The revolution never ends, he's got it figured out: it lingers like a rust around the heart. It waits, yes, but down the street, as if by order, grinds the garbage truck, the slop tank no less, and the poor bastard who rides in back, glides from his hold to sling another bucket up . . . *O Lord, vood ja look dar* . . . and slumps, suddenly brought low, gut-punched by the stink of us all, puking like a child. It's true, comrade, our wretched sufferings are a shame. The driver waited in the cab, embarrassed, eyes in the mirror, five minutes maybe, while our friend stood there spitting at an elm tree, till it was time he must have figured to get back to work.

for Eric Johnson

ELECTION YEAR

Out of what muck
had he struck out,
trailing flags of algae
the color of oil,

how far had he drug
his rune-drawn shell
across the wards,
munching their fetid,

green fusings, their
wary pedestrians?
He wheezed,
a hissing mud might make

if mud could walk.
I flipped him over,
I read his past—
road maps and

stratagems of real estate,
a sodden suburb
claimed by flood.
Quick to piss,

he snapped his neck
back in his collar.
No money here.
He left to work

the parish fair,
pumping fatty
from his hustings
in the swamp.

THE NOVEL IN THE GARDEN

All winter the pecan spends nothing, old man
saving his name from the bank and the children,
the lumpish brats no sonnet could control.

And now it's March, neither leaf nor news,
another month lost waiting on the check.
How many drinks before that Rapunzel

can't remember. A cools sun spills
under the skirts of the cedar: A touch
of castle fever, and now a tear, no bigger

than a nut she's cried so many. She makes a wish—
a prince perhaps with a touch for numbers,
an accountant she could train—and stumbles

back between the pages, between the briars
and peppermint camellias, a spool of sun
to spin her way, happy to find her bed,

a spectacle of fiction.

THE COBBLER'S JOURNAL

Shoes, boots, women's handbags, nylon awnings,
leather mitts and gloves, my uncle's brogans,
the spats my sister wore in high school.

We are the two people in the world
with a mole under the arch of our left foot.

––––––––

Nothing surprises me. I love your twelve toes.
Such nerve. Such balance.

––––––––

V said she had fallen in love.
I'm sure it's a woman.
She loves my tiny feet.

––––––––

I have never put my tongue in anyone's shoe.

––––––––

I sleep in my shop near the bars,
the footsteps belong to no one.
The fights, I hear them start:
You sonofabitch, I'll fix your shoes!

––––––––

 In bed my feet argue the direction of my death.

––––––––

Footprints near my pillow.
A note: *Gone to Belize for sandals,*
fear sleep till I return.
I wonder how she travels,

her footprints are not winged.

————

What I secretly wanted each Christmas:
the brushes, the tins of Brown Kiwi,
a job at The Club.

————

Father, I was lying when I wore your shoes.

THE CYCLIST'S PREMONITION

In the shapes of cars—silver figurines
the petit fours revving up the boulevard

a box of crackers on wheels,
a soup can fished from the dump,

meaty wedges that'd bust the ice on Willow Pond,
clubs you'd never wield against your brother,

but here it comes blowing up beside you,
air-horn ashy draft of cave mouth

come to swallow you up, fair rider,
shaking in the turn lane to the dead.

for Wm. Stafford

III The Bad Caddie

U-HAUL

Because he'll be taking nothing with him,
not the flower boxes stuffed with phlox,
not these melon-red camellias,
not the fence the dog would straddle,
the estate sod of the neighbor's lawn
where he would land, tripping security—
STAY WHERE YOU ARE, YOU WON'T BE HARMED—
and not the rain (rotting calendars of rain!),
the thrill of flood, unmoored houseboats lashed
to light poles, police jurors wading past their knees,
highwater marks chalked in river flush they tiptoed to reach,
where even now among the willows across the levee
he'd feel just a nose, one good breath above it all.
And *it.* What was it? What held him refusing to forgive,
turning always his reedy look upon them,
wanting in those faces behind the window
some gesture of regret, one hand rising
in a wave against the glass?

ASH WEDNESDAY

The duende never repeats himself . . .

He let go, an actor in a last, reluctant exit,
a long held breath, tugging his weight
from the balls of his feet as if there were something
stuck there, something he said, something
he kept stepping in, mayonnaise or love,
lingering like a ghastly abstraction,
one of those desserts he spit behind the curtains
when the hostess turned her back.

She stood at the window checking her shoes.

Someone a bit too drunk had climbed the roof
to wave goodbye, or hurry him along,
as if the bad parade would finally pass
and what they had caught they could throw away:
rougy cups, the coconuts, the paper crowns.
There was a satchel of ash left by the curb,
the coroner's predictable smirk,
graffiti smeared in a petri dish,
lonely one liners all in a row.

for Randal Wilson

Pan Olympic

On a spongy neoprene the ancient Greeks
would weep to race their callous-blasted feet

he goes striding off, already daydreaming,
checking the time, the calculus of track and wind,

the odds against the field, his friend up there,
the company runner, the one in black sweats,

side-stitched, as certain as an apparition,
there in the last lanes reserved for walkers.

Around and back as if to get it right
he runs inward from lethargy and age,

one lane, one lap at a time, centripetal
argument for order, down the eight lanes,

each quarter faster, cleaner, more pattern.
He merely sews the border, circling closer,

reaching to where his hand could trace
the naked joy in cosine arc of cloud

and steel—*ah god,* he breathes, preserved
by breath, the body's pennant, barely

audible: here in the sunstruck dewy glare
of academia, how lucky he should feel,

like something precious under glass.

ROLL CALL, THE MUNY LINKS

Action Jackson   Barley Pop   Beerless   Beware of Doug
Bird*   Boudin   Bugs   Butcher   Chandelier
City Pool   Colonel   The Commissioner
Drunken Duncan   Duck Lips   Elmo   Farticus
Flutter Valve   Five Times   Gravel Pit*   Heeb
Hook   Hot Tub   Ice Man   Ice Nine   John Rickles
Jr. Broom   Killer*   Lighthorse   Lips   Mayor*
Menace   Ming*   Nater   Otis   Pants (the Grunt)*
Party Man   Plumber Gone Bad   Princess Y
Puff   Purple Haze   Queerless   Razor   ShopDog*
Soup Bone   Sponge   Strange   Sweet Willie   Tarp
Taylor Made   Tel Star   Toe   Total Package
Uncle Tom   Volero   Walnut   Whiskey
Wildebeest   Xed Out   You're Wrong   Zoo Keeper

for Johnny Myers & Co.

CLUBLAND

More metronome than music, but it remains American,
the gang mowers chopping it up along the skirt of rough
where ClubLand's Walnut works the tune between his lips,
ciphering his options, calculating the press that would deliver him
even, owing no one, something that must feel like rapture
or birth or, for Walnut, the odd chance that Reagan returns,
yodeling a cardboard refrain cut out of the movies.
In the buggy you don't see the shanks, the yanky putts,
just the numbers circled up big and round, a defilade

of snowmen. When he goes three down,
he quits with the whistling, *purple rain, body and soul,*
and nothing left in the bag but nicotine and bologna,
remnants of the Delhi Dixieland Catfish Open & Calcutta,
all bones and bogey grease. They go to whip-it on the back side,
a little huddle behind the tenth grabbing at the cash,
one hand gloved, the other just a fistful of primitive flesh
clutching a ball . . . and The Little Nut's nerves about to snap,
big valve, big valve, open the big valve . . . and Rock thinking

hookah hookah hookah hookah . . . and Champagne
lost in the pastoral scores of inconsequence, in the stillness,
in the interstitial opiate upon which all sport depends:
See it settle through the long arm of the fairway,
flooding zoysia, azalea, the bloody myrtles at the lip
of the berm dimpled with broken acorns and cigarettes
slashed by the mowers and the rodents in their noisy wake
who go squirting for the shade . . . Waggle and crack!
O what'll it be? Popup-powerfading-doublecross overing-

duckhooking-dribbling groundhog top—*Hop toad hop toad*—
something to chase and curse. The drama of it all.
And on the eleventh it rains the Scottish coast,
but they emerge untroubled, wrapped in trashbags,
dripping with foppishness, to the eighteenth where Ben Hogan
their lonesome hero paused fifty years ago, putter cocked
above a twenty foot eagle, to address the crowd,
lookalike Eisenhowers and June Lockharts, pleated and cuffed,
crisp from the mint, who'd come out to thank the man

for demonstrating his grace upon this little snowglobe
of the south, "Before I make this putt I thought I'd
thank y'all for coming out." And it butter-rolls to the hole,
inevitable as luck or the midterm elections,
but the ball of Walnut, forget the ghosts, stops a quarter
turn short and he falls, prostrate, peering into the cup,
the trumpet bell where ClubLand is tuning up,
is orchestrating the dead, where the past (*can you hear it?*)
has played and plays again. No matter how you vote.

BAD CADDIE'S LAMENT FOR THE MOTHERS

He remembers the processing plant, proud to dare
his bully friends to brace the wretched drafts
of chicken exhaust, proud to splatter his snowballs
against the gut truck as it pulled dripping out of the lot
on its way to some other paradise of slop, but he tells no one
what she went through to find something else:
the applications, the lies, towing him along

through every door, the manager at DuckIn ShortMart
who pulled her aside, pressing her history:
*Your job at Johnny Thompson's Chickens, could you
be more specific?* Bad Caddie's cue to duck out,
to inspect the counter wares, the whiskey pints,
sausage biscuits, the rack of photo whores—
for him she never paused or dropped her chin.
Butthole cutter, she answered, *topnotch butthole cutter.*

His Adolescence

It's still back there, stuck like the dimes
and ballpoint pens in the ceiling tiles above the gym.
he can't quite touch it though hand over hand he climbs,

entire 8th grade below, white shorts and flattops.
Look at him go, Coach says, *look at him go*.
Dizzy, he shinnies down the rope, spinning

like a pigeon in a crazy draft, like shoes
pitched through a bedroom window,
and the face in that window—it all comes back—

early insomniac, locust racket, stringy chords
lifting from the roadhouse near the edge of town,
the geared crescendos of far away diesels.

Friday nights, he followed in through
folding bleachers to lurk a greasy swamp
creased with light and sandwich wrappers,

quarters sparkling in a muck of gum
and mustard smear. They lunged at change,
on their knees crept toward the bright

thighs of cheerleaders flashing through the slats,
and if a season later they lagged behind,
pairing off behind the Lutheran School,

fumbling in the must of fallen leaves,
semen expiring in their pockets,
it wasn't, thank god, for love.

ARS POETICA

Don't talk to my ball while it's rolling.
-Gaylord Burroughs, PGA

As far as I can tell, the world had been
returned to the poets, but for what?

A rinse and detail? Renaming? I check
the ranks and find, well, actually just two,

me and call him anonymous, a man whose books
I'd proudly stolen. We met once at a party in Missoula

and Mr. Anonymous laughed at my shoes.
But never mind that, this is Montserrat,

my own screwy dream, in some ambiguous
moment of its drama: Are we the last men alive?

Is it a tragedy? It's hard to tell, certainly it looks like a joke,
the two of us shoveling with our cocktail plastic

from a yellow cement truck, our taxi from the bar
REM-morphed to this. One minute we're drinking,

the next we're plugging, if you can believe it,
this volcano, this natural fault in the world.

Hah! Alchemical fire, our last mission.
He thinks it's funny, appreciates the irony.

Beneath the ragged fog there rolls a smoky funk
as red as barbeque, but we won't be eating.

Like all our readers, anyone with any sense
has left, even the truck, the driver we never paid,

and still my fellow poet keeps talking. Poets.
If we could just fill it up he's telling me, seal it

tight as take-out plastic, but mail a little home,
he winks, a stash of muse to keep the basement lit.

Right. We're all alone, it's gonna blow, sure as
the smoldering, postmodern muck between my toes.

Another toast, he says—gypsum, clay, silica, lime
all pounded to a dust, gravel, water, sand—

one cup, then another, our champagne ready-mix
gone down the hole that leads to God,

that Great Gorilla who handles all the rent
in Kansas City. *Show me* I say. Over the rim

we listen for a splash; cups smack, flatten
like paper, flashing up through cindered drafts

until they read like—get this—poems, thick as canceled
bets from the track, or the lace-white hands

of child communicants. *It's the birth of metaphor,
certain death!* He knows that I know it's over,

et cetera, but he's breathing, a billowed saint, even smiling,
here at the end of the world. Yes, it is a tragedy.

Something is happening, he looks ready to leap.
And me? his eyes want to know. What about me?

Where are my shoes? Those ugly ones
with the blue tongues I used to think were cool.

I'm turning around, barefoot in the ruts
left by the cab-cum-truck backing away, back to

Missouri. I'm going home. Leave me to my prosaic plot
there above the Bootheel, in the state of my art,

slacker that I am.

THE BAD CADDIE

You were born to waste your life.
-Louis Simpson

Maybe you should go for a walk,
take your shoes from the dog's mouth,

leave a tip, get powdered,
spend the day looking for lost balls
in the high rough

running down Country Club Road,
numbers three, thirteen—cave hole!—
the dogleg (no relation) ninth.

Then the long climb to the unclaimed lots,

out there along the edge of what
the more experimental republicans

call wilderness
(the ditches I mean) and where by contrast

you feel best, sunk as you are up to your nuts
and beating with a titanium wand

this godsown welter of matter & facts: the nature and
waste, effluvium et cetera,
one finds at the borders of a board game
writ such as this:

wilted azaleas,
cocktail plastic, the mower's shed,
the hand opening to receive its tip,

chemical trauma,
the boneyard of old pros,
red by-god American ants:
the basic elements of the universe
(in translation):

Bic lighters, abandoned carboys,
the flatulent half-life of the disposed.

What memories! Balata rubber, ink, all
but a few bites of a radar burrito, a wrinkled napkin
kissed with a belch: The pick of the litter, my man,

51

for sale as far as you can see,
a fairway near the dump, a future.
                                        Think about it,

some where to love:
                              its corners claimed, the half-pint somersaults
              in a flattened parabola
                            above the Riviera's busted taillight,
        a last-prayer hook shot missing wide,
            exploding in a wreck of whiskey light
against an empty quart of Busch:

      and in that spark is born your love,
                            distilled, full-lipped, wanting more.

  Call it luck,
                    you call it a wand,
          it looks more like the left-handed
wedge from your father's bag
            rotting slowly there in the basement,
                              a bag of shag balls
idling in the ooze. From a distance (and I can't tell you
      how important perspective is here)
because you're short and thin,
                              you look
a little weedy, unsheltered,
      a long walk from a rain shack
          (if you know what I mean)
should it come a sudden hail of birdie dust.

      It's a contact sport, occasionally toxic.
                        (Upon hearing the shouted "fore,"
the player should cup his hands behind his head,
      covering the ears, eyes the temples,
and never look up.)

      Keep your head down, wear a cap.
                                You're a man of impossible lies,
and by all estimations and actuaries,
          just another goofy bastard beside the road,
  suffering in the trash for us all,

stepping from behind a tree, zipping up,
spilling the rocks from his shoes,
his sack full, a Dump Family Singer wandering
his way out of it all, whatever it was
he wanted to say: *I once ate a shoe.*

See:
there's nothing to say. No movie, no movie credits,

but quite a racket
released from the last row of Mercer's Theater, 1965,
golf balls, by the buckets, all galloping
toward the screen at just the perfect moment
in *Gone With the Wind,*
Rhett Butler whipping

a blinded mare for the collapse of a culture
burning there on the scaffold of Selznicks's
Hollywood set.
It was your best joke,

but who will defend these Titleists, Maxflis,
men of real distinction?
With your wand you beat them all,
anoint their ecstatic relocation,
Saint Catabolism,
the two-toned party balls (considered omens),
the Slazengers James Bond sliced to the heath,
a single Pink Lady
who weeps in your pocket.

Before you know it, the afternoon assumes
its shape, out and back,
a bit warped from round,
scuffed, smudged.
Liking the ruse, you lingered
like a salesman warmed by the sun,
offered for inspection your dimpled gems,
your lost anarchy, tattooed, minimally logoed,
inappropriate,

but loud enough to wake a ghost

(pick a president)
                    dozing there near the tee box,
            puzzled with the slow play, now awake,
                    caught between clubs
                                        (must he choose wrong?)
            a bit too happy with himself,
perfect statue of it all. He never knew what to say.

                    The cave hole, remember? A hard right
            through the pines, the hole that always
                    gave him trouble—two nine irons,
            maybe eights, an eight or a nine?

                    What will you tell him?
You're the bad caddie.
                    You're damned if you know.

                                        for James Crumley

A Short Lesson on the Grip

In the hands of the wrong
person, the club is too

light, too apt to trigger
the alarm to lost yearnings

that sleeps in the palm.
The trick is to

let the poison take,
let the linguists win,

let absolute paralysis
bind alloy and brain.

Hold it as you
would the hand

of a child grown
weary with your cautions,

there in the middle
of the street.

for Bryan Di Salvatore

55

BESTIARY FOR THE BACK NINE

When the tasseled green catkins tumbled
from the pecan and the pistillate stars flowered
in the black wind at the back of the range
and fell on the balls driven long from the tees
where the rough clambered free from the blades,
where the white grub tunneled the shuck of old nuts
and the skunk shuffled out of her maiden grass shack,
where the red ant read the grain of a swale,
where the heron leapt from roof of a cart,
where the fox crept out of his fable to cheat by himself,
where the buttermilk racer lapped at the divot,
where the wolves lounged in the frog hair
and the rats ran into the cup, where the blackbird
circled the flagstick, a scorecard stuck to his beak,
where the caterpillars mossed on catalpas,
where the slugs wormed down the thumb of a glove,
where the lady bug dripped from the tongue of a coon,
where the grackles gambled their scores in the live oak,
where the deer snacked on dwarf grass TifEagle,
where the possum shoved his snout through the head cover
and waddled blindly down the lawns of the suburbs,
where the aphids spat their honeydew chews,
where the crows lingered in the myrtles
washed in a lather of bogies,
where the moons in the creek were caddied by spiders.

IV The Supplicant

LUCK

You could see it in his eyes
before he cut the deck, the blue cards,
the rider-backed bicycles . . .

then the black and red runs of gin rummy,
the checkered Formica, the Knights of Columbus.
And nights we waited patient as a rosary

for headlights behind the curtains,
for his hands and the five-dollar smiles.
I took my split in BB loads,

stacked her games of solitaire. Thanksgiving,
the family priest dealt six-point pitch,
Hi Lo Off-Jack Joker Jack Game.

I called my father late for dinner—
547-4588—*come on the cornbread's in,*
and the cards always came around

like payday, like his *Lieber.*
547-4588, the numbers click and spin,
haunt the dial like busted odds

or a hand he held but out of town
he gutless folded. Who wins,
which horse, one chance in ten,

like cancer, or a love for life?
The gambler never sees the future,
his life is better wasted.

Near Viola

Down from this crossroads
the mule-eared magnolias clap with rain.
One stubborn silo sinks in kudzu.
Once burned, its barn keeps its promise
never to return. Not me.
I'm not counting the miles to thunder.

In a windy boast of rain
I can almost hear him laughing,
or slumped in a rocker, just dozing off,
dropped crossword, pecans clattering
at his feet.
           Look closely under the porch
and you'll spot his progeny, spellbound,
already making himself up,
his hands full of chicken spit.
Eisenhower . . . the goddamned Eisenhowers.
Listen. Daddy's talking in his sleep,
and the words fall into my lap,
however odd, run over my lips,
impossible to spend,
just like the house above.
Lilacs and bananas I remember,
coffee, tobacco, someone leading me
down another decade's peculiar dust,
yellow envelopes brittle with palsy
and the words of a nephew
shot the last day of the war
on the road to Paducah.

Last week his *Leiber* asked
and I couldn't recall Uncle Lubey
tossing me over the mule.
His Elgin heirloom doesn't run.
The tobacco barns have fallen in, his house
a snaky trap in someone's else's clover.
The past is always greener.

Somewhere behind this rain
my father's reaching for a Viceroy,
and ever the wakeful one
I watch the orange light
arcing from the ashtray to his lips,
my mother sleeping
under the warm smoke of his breath.

A Last Visit

In the room to which I keep returning, no matter how it is dimmed, I can still find his bed, the heirloom crucifix, the closet where the clothes in which he felt familiar wait to be worn again, where the accouterments of habit still play in the dreamy gaze we give to one another. It's the TV that lights the room. Without sound, the mute figures flash absurdly across our faces. He moves with attenuated humor and when he speaks, hushed by emphysema, the words hurt. It is so near the end, for us, for the body, when all the lines of principle and pride disappear like a field below a flood, whose waters hold if only for a moment my own reflection. I check my breath for tobacco. *I smell smoke*, he says, *please don't smoke.* He waves my lie away. I take his hand and hold it in my own, rub the old scars of the free thinker whose consent to baptism last week, he wants me to understand, he gave only to ease her conscience. Some things we will never forget, and some linger, by god, if for a moment then too long—on channel 30, the stay-puff preacher probes our sin, his eyes locked shut from prayer.

SADNESS THE GARDENER SOWS

It might have been the first day of spring
but he didn't feel like telling any lies.

The spinach leapt in little bows.
There was the business of thinning,

deciding which would fill their stomachs.
He had a birthday in mind, late April,

a picnic on the patio, the tomatoes
just beginning to flower, a light vinaigrette,

orange nasturtiums, which they would
pop shyly into their mouths,

laughing like bees among such wealth.
The thinned sprigs he tossed to the mulch.

The grass still wore its ragged look,
like a child running the river's bluff,

daydreams of play twisted in his hair.
See him enter the house in late afternoon,

a Sunday, his parents napping. He is so quiet,
holding his shoes, placing each foot

on the polished stairs. No one would wake.
There should be nothing a man will not forgive,

but how he regretted her look in the window,
such a worried face for a windy day.

DOMESTIC

Not long after you first walked
you danced, a crazy kind of penguin hop,
feet stuck to the floor, arms at your side,
as if holding weightless pails of ice,
flightless Antarctic joke, and how we laughed.
Ginger Baker, bluegrass, Sonny Rollins,
you even found the beat to Mahler's Ninth.
We slapped our butts and sang along,
capable, however compromised, of joy,
as in a Brueghel print, or so we thought.
It won't last long. Everything's about to change:
you've started picking up your feet,
and just today, you whirled a dizzy windmill.
On your back, you stared for us to lift you up
and we came stumbling to your need.

for Jake

Ginkgo Biloba, in Memoriam

Ancient tree
of the pagoda,

silver fruit
the Buddhist

blessed. Forgive us
our good intentions,

forgive us our
transplants, forgive us

our negligence,
the near killing dose

of Osmocote
and forgive Jake

running reckless
on the Barbie jeep.

In spite of us
you might lived

a thousand years,
waving your golden hands.

Home Improvement

　　They could read by the crayoned lines on the slab
where the bottom plate would run, the dimensions
of shower wall and vanity, circled drains and hookups,
and for a moment imagine the garage rinsed of all
its musky junk, their current abstraction swept
to a trash can beyond their worry, the future winking
from a nickel-plated fixture in the plumbing aisle at Lowes.

　　And then they couldn't. Confusion followed,
they went back to disagreeing for the evening . . .
you need a vanity all your own. Yes he said I do.
They might have but they didn't. In the landfill
of their sleep they dumped it all, blueprint and loan,
power tool and wallboard, level and cord. Remodeled,
they woke in a dusty compost they recognized as home.

YARD SALE, *THE CHILDREN'S RUG SHOW*

Lost in cast-off, homey merchandise
a watercolor on cardboard,
                              unsigned and dated '76:
I almost miss it, but the splashy reds and desert blues
get you smiling.
                    Hung from looping entries,
on thick walls stuccoed the colors of cantaloupe rind,
      of mango past ripe, there must be twenty rugs,
but there are no children smiling back.
                  No grownups gawking about,
reaching for their wallets.
                              As if everyone had been poured
out of the painting, but step inside,
      it is the hour before the gallery's opening,
                              On the outer wall
a rug with predictable stick figures,
      bright African stripes, steely cats, three-pronged palms
with red fruits slung low, baskets and a two-legged burro,
            even a title—*Happy Bounty*!
            and there are children waving,
      but without hands. Stumpy arms end at the sleeves,
open wide like the exaggerated postures of semaphore.
            A boat stilled on a thumb of lake,
azure mosque, everything topped with a little Byzantine hat.

      Still the children oddly look about
      for someone's hand to hold:
                  Their ranging playgrounds
of thought, never hiding anything,

            for long. Apprise the sculpted lumps of Play-Doh:
trash or treasure. Meta-land model and make believe
      and what the artist would have seen . . . I wonder if these rugs
were ever woven, ever hung against these walls.
                              No subterfuge
      in what your brother paints—misaligned planets lit
with sunny fruit and frogs whose attitudes never depend
      upon your own.

This morning, little critic, remember?
    you crowded near his easel.
        You thought it good enough to eat?
You bit your theory on his thumb.
                                The Primal

    Primary-Colored Scream.

So when I lift you up to see the rugs
                I'm already leery,
you're ready to bite. This rug-woman's hair is stiffer than a skillet.
        Her chickens, pigs and cows go
            whirling round her head.
Her nearest arm aches right out of her heart,
      the fingers perfect, but the other, the hand
          that feeds us all, is
                    scarred and clawed.
    Is that its art?

       Retreating inward, the rugs diminish room by room.
    They look innocent enough but there
      that cat's all wacked, red with lightning stripes.
It's more than paint. His blue eyes burn
      like pepper down my throat.
                    Ten bucks,
    we'll haggle down the patron.
      It needs a frame.

                        for Emerson Marie

More Food for the Materialist

After supper we sit
on the back stoop,
the blue dusk of early spring

spread out before us,
budding tulip, pink crocus,
like something catered.

How full we were of winter
and its chicken-bone
nostalgia. Now the moon

rising slowly from his seat
to join us, to add a word
or two, a fat man come

to bless the long buffet,
crumbs on his collar,
cheese in his teeth.

Look, we beckon to Jake,
see the man in the moon.
For all our silly spoof,

he never tires of us,
our gallant toddler.
We point again,

see the man in the moon?
But now he's puzzled,
I see . . . he pauses, looking hard,

enamored of the metaphor,
I see a man feeding a dog.
How we applaud.

Not three years old
he retools our ready myths,
our charm. And across

the alley our neighbor
fills his beagle's dish.

BIRTH ORDER BLUES

Hang onto your doughnuts . . .

Each child is a riddle, something of a Sphinx—
four legs, two legs, three legs—but you, Whistling Westly,
Tubby T. "Sweet Cream" Butter,
you started shaking your leg way too early.

> *it keeps on going up*
> *it's never never gonna stop*
> *it keeps on going up*
> *never never gonna stop*

On the long road north to grandma's
through the picked delta speckled with blackbirds
lifting in a chorus from the cotton stalks,
you rolled out whole albums from the backseat,
Cow Blues, The Creamed Corn Blues, Crows,
spontaneously combusted, till we begged
for you to stop.

> Some nights
your lastborn, precocious sadness wouldn't leave you alone
although she tried her best to "put you down."

> *But Momma I don't ever want to grow up*
> *I know we're gonna die*

The blues needs a mother, it never knew a father,
someone to hear it out and not say no.

How I lay awake, listening for the slightest creak
of bedsprings, for her lovely footfalls on the stairs
through the kitchen and down the hall.

THE MAP

What was it we left behind?
There were other rooms from whose windows
we watched barefoot children playing in the rain.

There was a prelude of glances to which we had turned,
a dusty vase on the mantel, no bouquet.
But I see now that I was right to have followed you,

that your beauty was merely a light
we reached for to enter this room,
where petals were spilling over the chair

and the end tables and the bed neatly made.
I know what we become.
I know a sunflower from a rug of ashes.

Before sleep your face darkens in the garden
where joy has grown and never grows old.

THE CAT SCAN

I slip into the lead jacket, tighten the lead collar,
and at last my worry wears its own weight,
has become something more than abstraction
or superstition as it did yesterday when I went
running and told myself if I could make five miles
the X-ray would find nothing, that his little head
would look as normal inside as it looks outside,
red hair and rusty freckles, dimpled, doughy cheeks.
Now he's fitted on the sled and will soon pass
through what looks like, he tells me, a doughnut,
his head a loaf of bread wedged in its tray.
He believes somehow it will make the pain
go away, and how can I explain otherwise,
even mention the word tumor, a word
so thick it loads the air above our heads
if we work the courage up to call its name.
I answer his question *why* a hundred times a day,
why for instance do we have to eat and why
in sleep we dream some things we'll never do.
I no longer count my white inventions lies.
He's holding still, trying even not to blink.
How much he respects us all, our instructions,
technologies, my half-cooked approximations
about how this world works. How fast it leaves
us all behind with few ideas to offer in return.
He's given his blood without a wince and
now the technicians withdraw, the terrible
whirring begins, the ticks and clicks which trace
this other truth about our lives. He slides forward,
red lasers mark his face, and I'm holding fast,
my hand locked around his ankle, my fingers crossed.

THE SUPPLICANT

Even though you answer the fine print,
include the footnotes of hazardous admission,
recant the litanies of denial,
you'll never come
to the end of your one little lesson.
Names, alibis, reparations.
Length of stay?
Consider a month,
consider briefly the doghouse afterlife,

something remodeled for the post-Christian,
more institution, as wide as purgatory,
the hymnal thrum of ash,
the tenured dead never really with it
shuffling like dropouts on methedrine,
nodding as the weather knocks.

One trims his beard in the rain,
one's forgotten his one regret,
and one's holding his place for me,
who can do nothing more this morning
than stare through this window,
prepare my apology, surely misplaced,
surely misunderstood in this body.

Under the crab apple our three-legged retriever
chases her tail, flashing from shade to light.
She skids on linoleum but does she recall
the car or the vectors of impact,
the brakes locking, that moment,
one second, the premonitory
glance up from the text? Or the backdoor,
blood-smeared, dusty blood in the crawlspace,
some vague instinct of embarrassment,
as if dying were something to hide,
a bluesy guilt we're taught to keep
all bottled up, to erupt
in gesture, hopefully redemptive—
our neighbor Oscar

holding her all the way to the vet's,
   A face extending forgiveness,
  the blessing of a toast?

 Last night, always a last night,
   said worthless argument left inside,
 I sat petting her three good legs,
     waiting for the storm I could hear building
like a cattle drive over Texas.
 The wind rolled over me, apple-blossoms
    tossed and fell, then the rain,
 a rodeo of hail and light. In the quiet
I held for a moment the last crust of winter,
  like a crow on my tongue.

 Water-logged, the morning paper
    lingers on the porch: item, page 3,
thirty-six out of one hundred Americans
  report that God has spoken to them:
        page 5,
 last week, on a lake near Shreveport,
one happy boater, balanced on his ski boat's prow,
  arms out-stretched against a storm,
   cried *Take me Lord, I'm waiting,*

 and the lightning nailed him right between the eyes.
  Or so the story goes.

Photo by Emerson Heflin

JACK HEFLIN's first collection of poetry, *The Map of Leaving*, won the Montana First Book Award. His poems have also appeared in many journals, including *The Antioch Review, Poetry Northwest, Nimrod, Willow Springs, the Missouri Review, Green Mountains Review* and *Poetry East*, and in several anthologies, including Sarabande books' *A Fine Excess: Contemporary Literature at Play*. He has been awarded Writing Fellowships from the Missouri Arts Council, the Montana Arts Council, and the Louisiana Division of the Arts. In 2008, the Louisiana Endowment for the Humanities awarded him an Individual Achievement in the Humanities. He is an Endowed Professor of English at the University of Louisiana at Monroe where he co-directs the creative writing program and co-edits *turnrow* and *turnrow books*.